English Song
Renaissance to Baroque

High Voice

Edited by Steven Stolen and Richard Walters

On the cover: William Hogarth, British, 1697-1764, *The Enraged Musician,* engraving on ivory laid paper,
1741, 42 x 55.5 cm, Restricted gift of Mr. and Mrs. Joseph R. Shapiro, 1992.1
© 1996, The Art Institute of Chicago, All Rights Reserved.

ISBN   978-0-7935-4632-9

HAL•LEONARD®
CORPORATION
7777 W. BLUEMOUND RD. P.O. BOX 13819 MILWAUKEE, WI 53213

Editors' Preface

We have suggested ornamentation that is stylistically appropriate, as well as being vocally comfortable for most singers. The songs are perfectly acceptable without ornamentation. The printed suggestions, always in smaller sized notes, will be a starting place for some singers. There are many further possibilities. Any ornaments and melodic embellishments should be pursued with complete regard to the individual singer's voice and comfortability. In embellishing the music of this period the melody can be decorated, but not obscured in the singer's ornamentation. The aim is to create spontaneity and a spirit of improvisation in a performance.

As a general guideline, in strophic songs ornamentation is added in later verses, particularly in refrains. In *da capo* arias ornamentation is added on the repeat of the first section of music.

Contents

As the son of an upholsterer, coffin maker, and erstwhile Handel opera producer, **Thomas Arne** (1710–1778) was part of a colorful and musical family. Arne gave his sister and younger brother voice lessons, and his wife was also a singer. His illegitimate son, Michael, was a composer and wrote the famous song "The Lass with the Delicate Air." Arne played lute and violin and was a self-taught composer. He had strong interest in the stage and had tremendous success as a composer of operas and masques. The song "Rule, Britannia" was from his masque *Alfred*, written in 1740. Other notable compositions include *Rosamond* (1733), *Dido and Aeneas* (1733), *Comus* (1738), some twenty-five books of songs, and numerous instrumental works, often featuring organ or harpsichord. In 1744 he was appointed resident composer at Drury Lane Theatre in London and held that post until a disagreement with a singer/actor prompted him to leave for Covent Garden in 1760. At Drury Lane, Arne received particular attention and acclaim for his settings of Shakespearean texts. He received an honorary doctorate from Oxford in 1759, hence the often-used title of Doctor Arne.

Little is known of **John Bartlet** (15??–16??), a man overshadowed both in fame and in ability by contemporaries such as Dowland and Gibbons. He seems to have been employed in the service of Sir Edward Seymour, Earl of Hartford, and received a B.Mus. degree from Oxford in 1610. A collection of lute songs that he published in 1606 contains his only known works.

John Blow (1649–1708) received his early education at the Magnus Song School in Newark. The early teacher of Henry Purcell, he was a chorister at the Chapel Royal in London. In 1668 he became organist at Westminster Abbey. He succeeded Pelham Humfrey as Master of the Children at Chapel Royal in 1674 and held that position until his death. Blow also returned to his position as organist at Westminster Abbey following Purcell's death in 1695. Blow's greatest contributions to the vocal repertory come from his service music, with over 100 English anthems, numerous welcome odes, five odes for St. Cecilia's Day, coronation anthems for James II and for William and Mary, and odes for the deaths of Queen Mary (1695) and Henry Purcell (1696). Blow also composed a masque, *Venus and Adonis* (1685), and a collection of songs, *Amphion Anglicus* (1700).

In addition to his contributions as a composer, **Thomas Campian** (1567–1620) was a well-known and widely traveled scholar, physician, and theorist. In 1605 he received his M.D. from the University of Caen and began practicing medicine in London. Much of his early creative years were as a poet, and his verses were set by many of his songwriting contemporaries. His first collection of ayres (with works by Philip Rosseter) was published in 1601, and four more collections were published between 1613 and 1617. In 1613 he published a book on counterpoint, and he had many of his poetic works, including the poetry in *Songs of Mourning*, on the death of Prince Henry, set by Coprario. Campian the composer set only his own texts, employing a simple approach to the vocal line, so as to preserve the poetic meter.

With the creation or invention of the "ayre" **John Dowland** (1563–1626) stands at the forefront of early composers of song. The ayre is a simple form where the primary interest is in the top voice. The other voices are usually written in choral style and could have been sung in that fashion, but were preferably performed by solo voice and lute. Dowland was both singer and lutenist and traveled widely, performing his music and learning about art and style throughout Europe. His early years were marked by a period of service in Paris, working for the English ambassador, Henry Dobham. In 1580, while in

Dobham's service, Dowland converted to Roman Catholicism. He returned to England in 1584, married, and tried to gain a position in Elizabeth's court. Unsuccessful, he began a period of travel that lasted until 1609, including time in Germany and Italy. Near the end of the century, Dowland returned both to Protestantism and to England, but again was unsuccessful professionally, so he went to Denmark as court musician to Christian IV in 1598. Dowland often complained of his lack of success in England because of his acceptance abroad. It was, however, his cosmopolitan background that made his music widely known and gave it such lasting impact. His works include three volumes of lute songs (1597–1603), a set of instrumental pavans entitled *Lachrymae*, and a collection of songs with viol and lute accompaniment, *A Pilgrimes Solace*.

Thomas Ford (1580–1648) entered into the service of Henry, Prince of Wales, in 1611 and was appointed one of the musicians to Charles I in 1626. "Since First I Saw Your Face" is from an anthology published by Ford in 1607 called *Musicke of Sundrie Kindes*. In addition to lute songs, the collection features catches, rounds, and other pieces intended to be performed by four voices. The work was sold in St. Dunstan's Courtyard, Fleet Street, the home church of many lute song composers of the time.

Orlando Gibbons (1583–1625) came from a musical family in Oxford. His grandfather Richard was a chamberlain of the city, and his father, William, was well known as a musician. At the age of twelve, Gibbons joined the choir at King's College, Cambridge, where his brother Edward was master of the choristers. In 1605 he was appointed organist at the Chapel Royal and held this position until his death. Oxford awarded him a doctorate in 1622, and he was appointed organist at Westminster Abbey the following year. He died suddenly at Canterbury while waiting to render his services at the marriage of Charles I. More notable as a keyboard player and composer for harpsichord and organ, and for his service music and anthems, Gibbons was a fine writer of madrigals in the traditional style. He left only thirteen in a published collection (1612), of which "The Silver Swan" is the most famous. Although originally written in five-part choral form, it has become a solo song in the tradition of the lute ayre.

George Frideric Handel (orig. Georg Friedrich Handel; 1685–1759) received his early training on the harpsichord and violin in Halle, the city of his birth. His first productions, of the operas *Almira* and *Nero*, were mounted in 1705 in Hamburg. Handel was a cosmopolitan man and traveled Europe—specifically, Italy, from 1706 to 1709. These years marked the successful premiere of the opera *Agrippina* (1709) in Venice, as well as the oratorio *La resurrezione* (1708) and Handel's emergence as a virtuoso organist and harpsichordist. In 1710 he assumed the position of Kapellmeister to the Elector of Hanover, but obtained leaves of absence for trips to London. When the Elector of Hanover became George I of England in 1714, Handel decided to stay in London for good. He founded his own company, the Royal Academy of Music, in 1720, and in 1726 became a British citizen, officially changing his name to George Frideric. The popularity of John Gay's *The Beggar's Opera* in 1728, combined with the competition from Italians like Bononcini, undermined Handel's early operatic success, and he went bankrupt. In the 1730s he turned to the oratorio and was tremendously successful. *Esther* (1732) was followed by *Deborah, Saul,* and *Israel in Egypt*. *Messiah* (1742) and the twelve oratorios he composed thereafter further ensured his security as a composer of oratorio. The oratorio more than made up for his financial losses as a composer and producer of operas, and Handel was a wealthy man at the time of his death. Individual arias from his operas and oratorios have had perennial appeal, and although they were originally composed for specific voices and characters, many have transposed easily to become a traditional part of the song repertory and suitable for any voice.

Although **Tobias Hume** (1569–1645) is known as a composer, he considered himself an amateur in this area and was in truth a full-time soldier. Despite his protestations, Hume was an excellent gambist and wrote two collections of viol music and songs (*Musicall Humours and Poeticall Musicke*, 1605 and 1607). His peculiar and eccentric personality has led historians to believe that he was the model for the character Sir Andrew Agrecheck in *Twelfth Night*.

Robert Johnson (1583–1633) was the son of lutenist and composer John Johnson. He was appointed lutenist to James I in 1604 and retained that position under Charles I. In addition to his lute songs, Johnson provided music and songs for stage works, including Shakespeare's *The Tempest* and Fletcher's *The Mad Lover*.

Robert Jones (1565–1616) was a noted composer of Jacobean ayres (later known as ballads). Between 1600 and 1610 he had five books of ayres and one book of madrigals published. Unhappy with his lack of success, he changed artistic directions and went into business with colleague Philip Rosseter to train young actors and promote Children of Whitefriars, a children's acting troupe.

Henry Lawes (1596–1662), like many other lute song composers, was a singer and served as Gentleman of the Chapel Royal. In 1634 Lawes composed the music for Thomas Carew's masque *Coelum Britannicum* and was commissioned by the Earl of Bridgwater to do the same for Milton's *Comus*. He always showed a fondness for great writing and was a friend of Herrick, Walter, and Suckling and was, in 1645, the subject of a sonnet by Milton. In 1636 he was selected to write music for the king's visit to Oxford and later that year had the first of over 350 songs for voice and continuo published. Other works include an opera, *The Siege of Rhodes*, service music, Christmas songs in Herrick's *Hesperides*, and an elegy on the death of his musician brother, William.

Best known as the organist at St. Peter's, Cornhill (the "actor's church" in the City of London), **George Munro** (1685–1731) has not been accorded high standing as a composer. Nevertheless, "My Lovely Celia," easily his finest and most enduring song, has for centuries been a staple of the vocal repertory. Primarily a keyboard player, Munro was also a composer of popular songs, mostly during his time as harpsichordist at Goodman Fields Theatre.

Like many of his colleagues, **Thomas Morley** (c. 1557–1602) began his musical life as chorister, singing at St. Paul's Cathedral. He was an early pupil of William Byrd and received his music degree from Oxford in 1588. At about the same time, he became the organist at St Giles's Church, Cripplegate, in London. In 1589 he was appointed organist at St. Paul's, and in 1592 he became a Gentleman of the Chapel Royal. Morley, who lived in the same parish as Shakespeare, in 1599 provided the music to "It Was a Lover and His Lass" for *As You Like It*. His treatise *A Plaine and Easie Introduction to Practicall Musicke* was published in 1597. Morley was a well-known madrigalist and helped compile *The Triumphs of Oriana* (1601), a collection of madrigals in praise of Queen Elizabeth. He also composed service music in English and Latin, fancies for viols, and pieces for virginal.

Francis Pilkington (1570–1638) received a B.Mus. degree from Lincoln College, Oxford, in 1595. Also a clergyman, he took holy orders in 1612 and was ordained to the priesthood in 1614. A resident and chorister in Chester, his significant publications include a book of ayres (1604) and his second book of madrigals (1624).

From the time of John Dowland to the notable figures of the twentieth century, **Henry Purcell** (1659–1695) stands alone as the greatest British composer, and his death marked the end of any important musical contribution from an English composer for nearly 200 years. Like many of his contemporaries, he came from a musical family, which included his brother Daniel, an important composer of the period as well. Purcell was a chorister at the Chapel Royal at the age of ten. In 1673 he left this position and began his study with John Blow, succeeding him in 1679 as organist at Westminster Abbey. In these first years at Westminster Abbey, Purcell began composing in earnest and wrote his first music for a play, Nathaniel Lee's *Theodosius*. He went on to write music and songs for over fifty dramatic works. *Dido and Aeneas* (1689) was written for a production at a girl's school and was his only through-composed opera. The work remains the only real representative of the period still being performed as a regular part of the repertory today. Other operatic and semi-operatic works include *King Arthur* (1691), *The Fairy Queen* (1692), and *The Indian Queen* (1695). Other notable appointments during his brief career include service in 1682 as a Gentleman of the Chapel Royal, where he sang bass and served as one of three organists. He also became, in 1683, the Royal Repairman, to oversee who would build the new organ at Temple Church. In 1685 James II named him Royal Harpsichordist. Despite these court appointments, Purcell depended greatly on the theater for work, and his enduring legacy is found in those compositions. He did compose a large amount of church and service music, including the music for the funeral of Queen Mary in 1694. This music was performed at his own funeral just one year later. His vocal music includes the ode for St. Cecilia's Day *Hail, Bright Cecilia* (1692) and the songs contained in *Orpheus Britannicus*, a two-volume collection published after his death. He also wrote *Nine Fantasias* (1680), *Twelve Sonatas of Three Parts* (1683), *Musick's Handmaid* (1689) for harpsichord, and another collection published posthumously, *Lessons for the Harpsichord or Spinet, Suites No. 1–8*.

Although not a prolific composer, **Philip Rosseter** (1568–1623) was a close friend of the more notable Thomas Campian and John Dowland. He was appointed by James I as court lutenist and served in this capacity until his death. A simple, unpretentious composer, Rosseter also was an impresario of sorts, working with fellow composer Robert Jones for a group of child actors known as the Children of Whitefriars.

Have You Seen But a White Lily Grow?

words by Ben Johnson

Anonymous
early 17th century

*optional melodic ornamentation by the editors

Willow Song

Anonymous
early 17th century

Pastime With Good Company

Anonymous, 16th century
attributed to King Henry VIII

Thou Soft Flowing Avon

words by David Garrick

Thomas Arne

Thou   soft   flow - ing   A - von,   by   thy   sil - ver ___
The   love - strick - en   maid - en,   the   sigh - ing   young ___

stream, ___ Of things more than mor - tal thy Shake - speare would ___

swain, ___ They rove with - out dan - ger, and sigh with - out ___

dream, ___ would dream, would dream, thy ___ Shakes - peare would

pain, ___ and sigh, and sigh, and ___ sigh ___ with - out

(tr)

dream. ___

pain. ___

[mf]

The fair - ies by moon - light dance round ___ the ___ green ___

[p]

* *The editors' optional melodic ornamentation is for verse 2.*

Blow, Blow, Thou Winter Wind

words from *As You Like It*,
William Shakespeare

Thomas Arne
1740

*In each of the verses, the two large sections
(measures 9-16, measures 17-32) may each be repeated.*

O Come, O Come, My Dearest

from the pantomime *The Fall of Phaeton*

words by Pritchard

Thomas Arne
1736

* *Dynamics throughout reflect tutti (b.f.) and continuo (b.f.).*

When Daisies Pied

words from *Love's Labour Lost,* William Shakespeare

Thomas Arne

1. When dai - sies pied, and vi - o - lets blue, And la - dy smocks all sil - ver white, And cuck - oo buds of yel - low hue, Do paint the mead - ows with de - light:
2. When shep - herds pipe on oat - en straws, And mer - ry larks are plough - men's clocks, And tur - tles tread, and rooks, and daws, And maid - ens bleach their sum - mer frocks:

The cuck-oo then, on ev-'ry tree, Mocks mar-ried men, mocks mar-ried men,

mocks mar-ried men; for thus sings he: Cuck-oo, cuck-oo, cuck-oo,

cuck-oo, cuck-oo! O word of fear, O word of fear, Un-

pleas-ing to a mar-ried ear, un-pleas-ing to a mar-ried ear.

* *optional melodic ornamentation for verse 2, by the editors*
** *appogiatura possible*

Whither Runneth My Sweetheart?

John Bartlet
1606

Tell Me No More

John Blow

[Moderately]

[mp]

Tell me no
more,__ no more__ you love; in vain,__ fair Ce - lia, tell me no

(tr)

more,__ no more__ you love; in vain,__ fair _ Ce - lia, in vain,__ fair _

Ce - lia, you__ this pas - sion _ feign. Tell me no more,__ no

more ___ you love. Can they pre - tend ____ to love, who do re - fuse what

love ___ per - suades ____ them to? Tell me no more, ___ no more ___ you

love. Who once __ has __ felt __ his ac - tive __ fire, __ dull laws __ of ____

hon - our will dis - dain. Tell me no more, ___ no more ___ you

love; in vain, __ fair Ce - lia you would be thought, you would be thought, you would be thought his

slave; and yet you will not, and yet you will not to __ his pow'r __ sub - mit.

Tell me no more, __ no more __ you love; in vain, __ fair Ce - lia,

[*p*]

(tr)

in vain, __ fair Ce - lia you __ this pas - sion feign.

Fair, If You Expect Admiring

Thomas Campian
1601

* appoggiatura possible
** *The editors' optional ornamentation is for verse 2.*

29

Jack and Joan

Thomas Campian

Weep You No More, Sad Fountains

John Dowland
1603

*The repeat is within each of the two verses.

Flow My Tears

John Dowland
1600

And tears, and sighs, and groans my wea - ry days, my wea - ry days
And fear, and grief, and pain for my de - serts, for my de - serts

Of all joys have de - priv - ed. Hark you sha - dows that in dark -
Are my hopes since hope is gone.

- ness dwell, Learn to con-temn light, Hap - py, hap -

- py they that in hell Feel not the world's de - spite.

What If I Never Speed?

John Dowland
1603

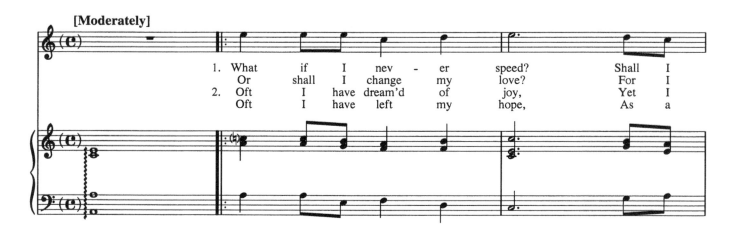

The Silver Swan

Orlando Gibbons
published 1612

The silver swan, who, living, had no note. When death ap-proach'd, un-lock'd her si - lent throat, Lean - ing her breast a - gainst the reed - y shore, Thus sang her first and

Since First I Saw Your Face

Thomas Ford
1607

The editors' optional melodic ornamentation is for verse 2 or 3.

Here Amid the Shady Woods
from the oratorio *Alexander Balus*

words by Thomas Morell

George Frideric Handel
1748

soul, this charm - ing seat, ___ Love and glo - ry's calm ___ re - treat.

Here a - mid the sha - dy woods, ___ Taste, my

soul, this charm - ing seat, Love and glo - ry's calm re - treat. ___

Here a - mid the sha - dy woods, Fra - grant flow'rs ___ and crys - tal floods, Taste, my

soul, this calm re - treat   Love and glo - ry's calm re - treat,   taste,_ my soul,   this charm-ing

seat,   love _ and glo - ry's calm_ re - treat,_____   love_____   and glo - ry's

calm _ (tr)   re - treat.

[*f*]

* *appoggiatura possible*
** *optional melodic variation by the editors*

Come and Trip It
from the oratorio *L'Allegro*

words by Jennens, compiled from Milton

George Frideric Handel
1740

*optional melodic ornamentation by the editors

Let Me Wander Not Unseen

from the oratorio *L'Allegro, il Penseroso ed il Moderato*

words by Jennens,
compiled from Milton

George Frideric Handel
1740

47

Where E'er You Walk
from the oratorio *Semele*

words by William Congreve

George Frideric Handel
1744

(optional notes are suggestions for da capo ornamentation)

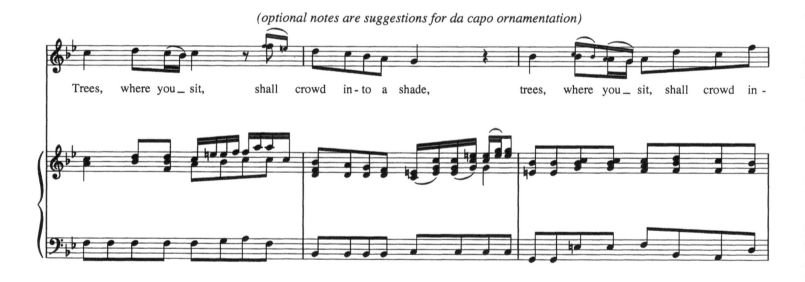

* *appoggiatura possible on da capo*

gales shall fan the_ glade; Trees, where you sit, shall crowd in - to a _ shade,_____

trees, where_you_ sit, shall crowd _____ in -

to ___ a shade.

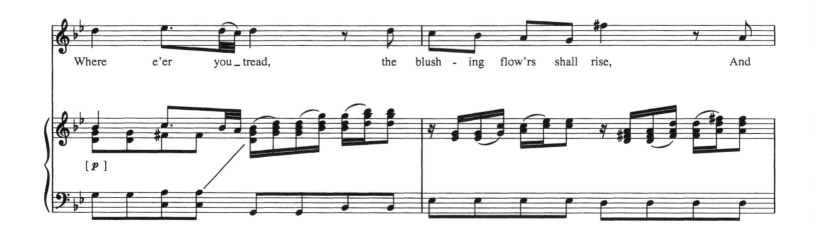

Where e'er you tread, the blush - ing flow'rs shall rise, And

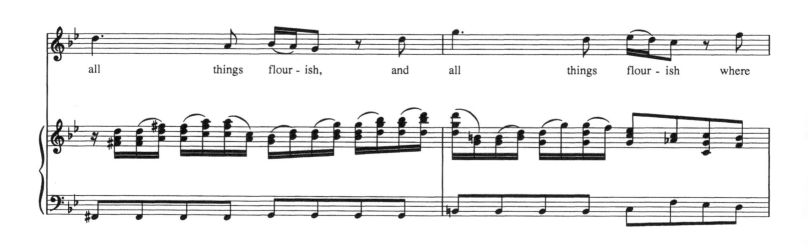

all things flour - ish, and all things flour - ish where

[Adagio]   Da Capo

e'er you turn your eyes, where e'er you turn your eyes, where e'er you turn your eyes.

As I Walked Forth One Summer Day

Robert Johnson
1659

Fain Would I Change That Note

Tobias Hume
1605

The editors' optional melodic ornamentation is for verse 2.

come, _____ Love is the per - fect sum _____
bliss, _____ Where tru - est plea - sure is, _____

_____ Of all de - light, _____ I have no
_____ I do a - dore thee. _____ I know thee

oth - er choice _____ Ei - ther for pen or
what thou art, _____ I serve thee with or my

voice _____ To sing or write. _____
heart _____ And sing fall be - fore thee. _____

appoggiatura possible

In Sherwood Lived Stout Robin Hood

Robert Jones
1609

first could hit a heart of his.
close - ly lodged in wo - men's eyes.
beyed - ness and a wink could win.
to the woods; Love fol - lowed me.

Hey! jol - ly Ro - bin,

Ho! jol - ly Ro - bin, Hey! jol - ly Ro - bin Hood! Love finds out

me As well as Thee To fol - low me, to fol - low me,

to fol - low me, to fol - low me to the green wood.

The editors' optional melodic ornamentation is for verse 3 or 4.

How Happy Art Thou

Henry Lawes

How hap - py art thou and I, That nev - er knew how to love!_____ There's no such bless - ing here be - neath What - e'er there is a - bove._____ 'Tis lib - er - ty, 'tis lib - er - ty That ev - 'ry wise man knows.

Out, out up - on those eyes That think to mur - der me, And he's an ass be - lieves her fair That is not kind and free._____ There's noth - ing sweet, there's noth - ing sweet To man but lib - er - ty.

I'll tie my heart to none, Nor yet con - fine mine eyes,_____ But I will play my game so well I'll nev - er want a prize._____ 'Tis lib - er - ty, 'tis lib - er - ty Has made me now thus wise.

My Lovely Celia

George Munro

The editors' optional melodic ornamentation is for verse 2 or 3.

It Was a Lover and His Lass

words from *As You Like It,*
William Shakespeare

Thomas Morley

* The editors' optional melodic ornamentation is for verse 3 or 4.

Rest Sweet Nymphs

Francis Pilkington

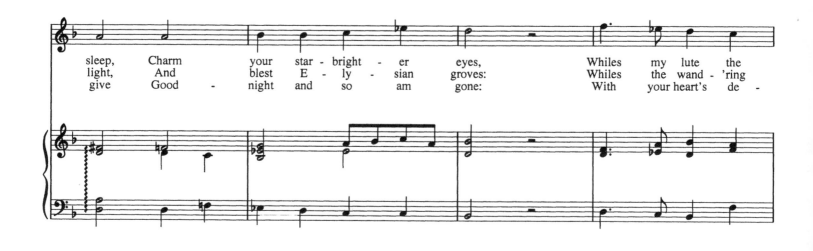

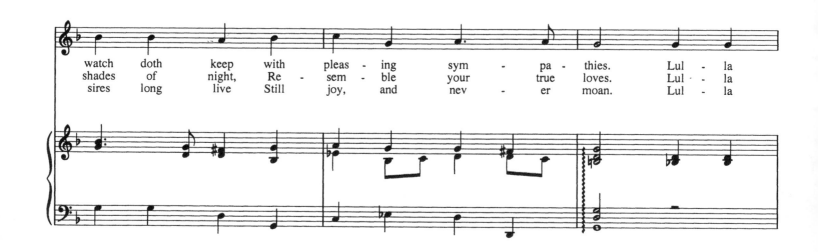

Diaphenia

Francis Pilkington
1605

This repeat within each verse, found in the original sources, is optional.

Nymphs and Shepherds
from the play *The Libertine*

words by T. Shadwell

Henry Purcell
c1692

now, now, now, now se - cure - ly__ rove_____ Whilst you ex - press, whilst

you ex - press_____ your jol - li - ty.

Nymphs and Shep - herds, come_ a - way, come a - way,

Nymphs and Shep - herds, come_ a - way, come a - way, come, come, come, come _ a - way.

optional melodic ornamentation by the editors

Hark! The Echoing Air

from *The Fairy Queen*

words by E. Settle,
after *A Midsummer Night's Dream*,
William Shakespeare

Henry Purcell
1692

Lyrics:

a tri - umph, tri - umph sings,

Hark! hark! the ech - oing air a tri - umph sings

hark! the ech - oing air a tri - umph sings, a

tri - umph a

* *optional melodic ornamentation by the editors*
** *appoggiatura possible*

tri - - - umph, tri - umph _ sings _____

_____ a tri - - - umph, tri - umph _ sings

And all _____ a - round, and all _____ a - round pleas'd _____

Cu - pids clap _ their wings, clap, clap, clap, clap _ their wings; pleas'd _____ Cu - pids clap their
[alt: pleas - - - ed _]

f

I Attempt from Love's Sickness

from *The Indian Queen*

Henry Purcell
1695

more now, no more now, fond ___ heart, with pride no more swell, Thou canst not ___ raise ___ for - ces, thou canst not ___ raise ___ for - ces e - nough to re - bel. I at - tempt from Love's ___ sick - ness to fly _____ in ___ vain. Since I am my -

* *optional melodic ornamentation by the editors*
** *appoggiatura possible*

I'll Sail Upon the Dog Star

from the play *The Fool's Preferment, or The Three Dukes of Dunstable*

words by D'Urfey

Henry Purcell
1688

* *Play slightly detached throughout.*

tear_____ the. rain-bow from the sky, I'll tear_____ the. rain- bow from the. sky, And tie,_____ and_tie_both_

ends to - ge-ther. The stars pluck from their orbs, too, the stars pluck from their orbs, too, And

crowd them in my bud- get! And whe-ther I'm a_ roar - - - ing boy,

a roar - ing boy, Let all,_____ let all_the_na - tions judge it.

If Music Be the Food of Love
(First Version)

Henry Purcell
1692

where. Plea-sures in-vade both eye and ear, so fierce, so fierce, so fierce, so fierce, the trans - ports

are, they wound, And all my sen-ses feast-ed are, And all my sen-ses feast-ed are; Tho' yet the treat is

on - ly sound, Sure I must per - ish by your charms, Un-less you save_____ me in your

arms. Sure I must per - ish by your charms, un-less you save_____ me in your arms.

* *appoggiatura possible*
** *optional melodic ornamentation by the editors*

When Laura Smiles

words attributed to Thomas Campian

Philip Rosseter
1601

* *The editors' optional melodic ornamentation is for verse 3 or 4.*